Culture, creativity and the young : developing public policy

by Ken Robinson

Cultural Policies Research
and Development Unit

Policy Note No. 2

Council of Europe Publishing

French edition :
*Une politique gouvernementale en faveur
de la culture, de la créativité et des jeunes*
ISBN 92-871-3856-7

The opinions expressed in this publication are those of the author and do
not necessarily engage the responsibility of the Council of Europe.

Cover © Jean Raty : photograph of a wall mosaic

Cover design: Graphic Design Workshop, Council of Europe

Council of Europe Publishing
F-67075 Strasbourg Cedex

ISBN 92-871-3857-5
© Council of Europe, April 1999
Printed in Belgium

Contents

Abstract

The future of Europe is its young people: their ambitions, sensibilities and values are the major foundations on which European development will be built. Young people are living in a world of immense and increasing complexities. At every turn the landscape through which they are moving is changing faster than at any time in history. This is true economically, socially and culturally. For all national governments there are two related priorities in planning for the future. The first is to find ways of realising the creative resources of all young people to enable them to participate in these changes positively and constructively. The second is to engage with cultural diversity while maintaining cultural identity and social cohesion. These concerns underpin the work of the Council of Europe's project " Culture, Creativity and the Young ". This policy note summarises some of the issues and proposals which have begun to emerge from the activities of the project to date. It draws from a survey of arts education in Europe published in the exploratory phase of the project (Robinson, 1997); from international colloquies organised by the project and from a series of thematic studies commissioned by the project's international advisory group. The note argues that it is essential for national governments to frame coherent policies and programmes to support the creative and cultural development of all young people, and it identifies the central questions and issues which will define these policies and the principles on which they might be based.

I. The context

The proposal for the " Culture, Creativity and the Young " project was developed at a preliminary meeting of a group of experts at the Council of Europe in autumn 1995 on the issue of the arts in education. The meeting was convened to discuss the recommendations of a background paper on Education and Culture (Robinson, 1995) for the Council of Europe's report for the World Commission on Culture and Development entitled *In from the margins*. The experts group agreed on the importance of developing the arts in education throughout Europe and that there is a pressing need for a system of exchange and co-operation among European states : to provide models of effective practice and to encourage the sharing of philosophies and experiences in the arts in general education.

The Culture Committee of the Council of Europe approved the establishment of a first working phase of such a new project which should concentrate on two main activities, thereby ensuring to cover all aspects of cultural provision for young people : an international survey (Robinson, 1997) and an international colloquy. The survey was carried out with the help of a questionnaire to the member states gathering information on current provision for the arts in formal education at primary and secondary levels. Supplementary information was compiled from published policy statements and curriculum guidelines from the contributing countries. The colloquy on " Culture, Creativity and the Young " took place in Varaždin, Croatia, in autumn 1996 and brought together professionals from twenty-five member states in the field of formal and non-formal education.

On the basis of these preliminary activities, a proposal was developed for a three-year action-research project. The objectives underlying the project were :

• to facilitate regional, national and international debate on the provision for the cultural and creative development of young people both inside and outside formal education ;

• to stimulate networking, the setting of partnerships and the exchange of information between governmental and non-governmental organisations ;

• to identify and encourage good practice in the field of arts education in the member states.

With a view to building the body of knowledge necessary to meet these objectives, four thematic studies were commissioned to renowned experts in arts education. The studies were to provide the theoretical framework and focus on key conceptual issues in cultural provision for the young, identify examples of good practice and draw out implications for policy and provision.

They were:

1. *The arts, commercial culture and young people: factors affecting young people's participation in artistic and cultural programmes* by Roger Hill (UK), in association with the Liverpool Institute for Performing Arts.

It is sometimes assumed that young people's lives are devoid of creative or cultural activities unless they are organised by " arts " professionals. Young people are continuously engaged in aesthetic and cultural activities through commercial and popular culture. What is the relationship between these experiences and those provided by arts and other cultural institutions ? Roger Hill looks at key issues of definition and argues for a revaluation of current policy based on a reassessment of the needs of young people themselves. He argues that the world of youth is seen as separate by both young people themselves and the rest of society but not for any stable or static qualities. Youth is understood as a time of action and reactions, a time when the future self is negotiated and an identity created which is open to continuous development. Young people strive for independence, hunger for new experiences, and struggle for certainties and a secure sense of identity. The arts can have crucial roles in these processes, but young people must be involved in shaping the policies that affect them.

2. *More, better, different : intercultural understanding and cultural diversity : the roles of cultural provision for young people* by Jennifer Williams (UK), in association with the British American Arts Association.

How can cultural provision for young people facilitate intercultural understanding within the member states ? This study considers the factors which are currently shaping arts and cultural policies and their implications for the development and empowerment of the young. It analyses changes within the arts and looks at how partnerships with other sectors, including education, social policy and business, can enable the arts to play a more substantial part in building democratic and sustainable communities. If member states are to make progress in promoting intercultural understanding, they will need to develop more specific policies for young people. Existing programmes in schools and communities should be built on and improved through involving young people in planning and evaluation.

3. *Working with young people: training of artists and teachers* by Carla Delfos (the European League of Institutes of the Arts – Elia, the Netherlands), in association with Euclid.

This study surveys the structures and methods for the training of artists and of arts teachers in five member states: Croatia, Finland, France, Italy and the United Kingdom. Information on other countries and on pan-European research and projects is also used to so as to provide a broader context for the study. The survey includes traditional forms of training in schools, colleges and other institutions; and non-traditional forms in youth centres, community centres, health related organisations prisons and so on. It identifies existing research into the training of artists and teachers and examines innovative projects using the arts, especially in non-traditional settings. The study makes a series of recommendations for future development.

4. *Reflecting on youth arts: towards a new framework to enable young people and the arts to come closer* by Michael Wimmer and Ebrû Sonuç (Austria), in association with the Österreichischer Kultur-Service, ÖKS (Austrian Cultural Service).

The term " youth arts " is used in a number of member states to refer to the involvement of young people especially in creating their own arts practices. This study looks at basic issues of definition and offers a survey of existing youth arts programmes in six member states : the United Kingdom, the Netherlands, Greece, Austria, France and Hungary. It reviews provision in the school system and raises fundamental questions about the effectiveness of this provision and of partnerships with a wide variety of cultural institutions. The study argues for a new framework for youth arts including new methods of funding and resourcing and for new approaches to education to transform schools into cultural centres. Key issues are raised about the roles of cultural institutions and about the implications of new technologies and new media for conceptions of arts practice. The study argues for new roles of teachers and artists and for new approaches to training in both fields.

The four studies analyse a wide range of issues. In many ways they agree, and in others they differ. This is to be expected in analyses of such dynamic, diverse and constantly changing areas of practice. Taken together, they do present important perspectives on issues which should be of central concern to all Council of Europe member states. The present policy note portrays the substance of these studies.

II. The challenges

Europe, in common with other regions, is struggling to engage with a catalogue of structural, demographic and cultural changes that are fundamentally transforming established ways of life. These challenges are :

Political

In the restructuring of Europe in the post-cold war period, established political boundaries are being redefined both as Europe strives to unify itself to face future demands and opportunities, and as historical communities assert their claims for political recognition and independence.

Economic

A major challenge for education systems is to equip young people with the knowledge and skills they need to make their ways in the increasingly complex world of financial interdependence and competition. The growth in new technologies, in particular, has created a world market for goods and capital that operates independently of national political boundaries. The long-established financial axis between the United States and Europe is shifting as the economies of the Pacific rim emerge as major forces in world markets.

Social

Economic systems and labour markets are being fundamentally changed by the accelerating innovations in information systems and technology. The shift from a production-based to a service- and information-based economy, necessitates people with much higher level skills than the schools are currently preparing. As a consequence of technological innovations, we are witnessing major changes in both the *nature* and the *rhythms* of employment and of unemployment in Europe. The new technologies are not only revolutionising commerce and industry, but are inflecting daily life with an avalanche of images. Individualism and moral relativism are replacing traditional beliefs. Many European societies are riven by exclusion and unemployment and for millions of Europeans promised " good life " is as far from reach as ever.

Cultural

Within Europe, there is an enormous diversity of cultural values and practices, within as well as between its member countries. European policy agreements, including Maastricht, have recognised the necessity of respecting cultural differences and commonalties within the process of pursuing common political and economic interests. Education must prepare young people to engage with cultural diversity as well as to develop their own senses of cultural identity in a world where values, identity and lifestyles are changing at an unprecedented rate.

National governments throughout Europe are seeking to engage with these challenges through, often fundamental, reforms to their state education systems. Arts and culture have not yet played a major role in cross-sector discussions about the future of communities. Citing the report *In from the margins*, Jennifer Williams argues that " there is a growing acknowledgement that, if culture – whether understood as the whole life of the people and its values, or more narrowly, as artistic activity of all kinds – is left out of account, sustainable development is likely to fail. "

In many national statements there is a dual emphasis in cultural policy. There is, first, a widespread emphasis on the importance of intercultural understanding and of mutual tolerance of different cultural traditions. This theme is elaborated the need to promote a wider sense of European identity. This appears not only in national statements but in a wide variety of intergovernmental agreements, most recently in Maastricht. The second is the need to promote a sense of national cultural identity and cohesion. [1] As Jennifer Williams notes in her study *More, better, different*, the key factor is the rapid pace of change.

> Among the changes are the growth in population, the speed of product development and the amount of readily available information. The conditions of our life on earth are fundamentally changing. The external complexity is increasing and as a result, the whole world is involved in making structural transformations to the way things work. What is emerging is a society which calls for networks rather than hierarchical management. In addition, there are pressures on governments to decentralise. Business is undergoing major reform. Educators are debating the shape and functions of future schools. The arts are re-examining their roles in society and there is a public discussion about what values will guide our actions in the next century.

In all European countries there is a growing concern that many individuals remain excluded from participation in the cultural life of their societies. Throughout Europe, many national and territorial minorities and other groups are denied their cultural identity. As Jennifer Williams puts it, a society that excludes cultural representation of any part of its whole memberships is impoverished. Moreover, the failure to resolve old problems associated with minorities and respect for culture differences has fuelled war and suffering on an immense scale. [2]

These transformations are profoundly affecting the lives of children everywhere. Some member states are taking the time to construct more fully developed policies to help ensure the economic, cultural and educational needs of young people are met. Apart from education very few sectors have developed sustained programmes of activity for young people.

Despite this, young people in Europe, no matter what their backgrounds are, speak more languages and are more mobile than the generations that precede them : they are more international in their thinking, more adaptable to change and more interested in diversity. They know more about the environment than any previous generation. She concludes that :

> Most youth work which focuses specifically on arts and culture is a relatively recent development. However, experiences of every scale do exist within Europe and elsewhere. The links with social work, education and with cultural organisations, the media and artists are among the areas in which youth arts work is expanding the most. Youth work connected with the arts is not only a growth area in terms of participation, but is also one of the only areas of youth work that tends to hold the attention of young people

over a period of time. Perhaps the greatest significance is the potential for arts and cultural activities to be linked to the development of good citizenship and other values within society.

III. A definition of the field

Culture and the arts

" Culture " has two meanings which are often blurred. It is used in a wide sociological sense to mean a given community's whole way of life : its economic, moral, religious, legal, familial, and aesthetic ways of being. It is also used to refer specifically to the arts. Dupuis (1995) refers to these as the " anthropological " and the " sectoral " definitions of culture. International debates on cultural development and co-operation tend to range well beyond the specific domain of the arts and their related fields of employment. In 1970, the Intergovernmental Conference in Venice acknowledged that culture was inseparable from everyday life and that it was equally important to take due account of the culture of science and technology. That conference also confirmed the global nature of the concepts of cultural, economic and general development and the fact that investment in the cultural sphere is long-term and " one of the factors which determine a society's success in development ". In 1972, Eurocult's recommendation No. 1 (Unesco, Helsinki) was more explicit. It stated that :

> Culture is not merely an accumulation of works and knowledge which an élite produces, collates and conserves in order to place it within reach of all, or that a people rich in its past and its heritage offers to others as a model which their own history has failed to provide for them ... culture is not limited to access to works of art and the humanities ; it is at one and the same time the acquisition of knowledge, the

demand for a way of life and the need to communicate ...
it is not a territory to conquer or possess but a way to be-
have towards oneself, one's fellows and nature. (Quoted in
Dupuis, 1995)

Culture, in these terms, comprises " the whole complex of
distinctive spiritual, material, intellectual and emotional features that characterise a society or social groups. It includes
not only the arts and letters are also modes of life, the fundamental rights of the human being, value systems, traditions and beliefs " (Dupuis, 1995, citing the preamble to the
Mexico City Declaration on Cultural Policies).[3]

The dual meaning of the term also points to the particularly
significant ways in which the arts help to express, formulate
and define the social culture. The experience of culture is not
of a number of separate and insulated spheres of social experience – the religious as distinct from the moral, the aesthetic as distinct from the technological – but of the dynamic
interactions between them. Artists do not live apart from the
cultural environment in which they work. It is through their
expressive insights in music, dance, literature, film, theatre
and all of the other modes of artistic representation that the
values and sensibilities of the social culture are shaped, chal-
lenged and defined. For these reasons an understanding of
the culture of a community is often best grasped through engaging with its achievements in the arts.

Popular culture

In public policy terms, the arts are often defined narrowly to
mean the experiences provided by public institutions : gal-

leries, museums, concert halls and theatres. [4] On this basis it is sometimes assumed that the lives of young people who do not attend these events must be culturally barren. A study for the Calouste Gulbenkian Foundation (Willis, 1990) argues that young people are constantly engaged in aesthetic, artistic and creative processes through their engagement with popular culture : a culture to which they contribute actively rather than passively consume.

> One thing is certain, for most young people, the traditional arts play very little part in their lives. Studies in this area suggest we re-phrase the questions we are posing : not how can we bring " the arts " to " the young ", but in what ways are the young already artists of their own lives ? Not exclusively, why is there culture not like ours ? ; but, what are their cultures like ? Not, how can we inspire the young with art ? ; but, how are the young already culturally energised in ways which we can reinforce ? Unlike the traditional ones, these new questions must be asked directly to the youth involved. (Willis, 1990)

Popular culture, by definition, is everywhere. It is multi-faceted and without a clear or single agenda. In his study on *The arts, commercial culture and young people*, Roger Hill argues that policy makers are likely to panic before the power of commercial culture but we do still retain policies and mechanisms for regulating its development. It is also easy to assume that what we cannot control is necessarily dangerous, but this is less so than we may think.

> Recorded music and images, broadcast and printed material, consumer items mainly made mechanically, live entertainment, digital information, games and recreations, edu-

cational aids, food and drink, travel and holidays, drugs and cosmetics – these are the language of commercial culture as spoken to young people, and listed in such a way they seem the very substance of life. They are however all in the end simply the products of private and public companies of various sizes and structures of management. An adult view of these products sees them as an ever-increasing mountain of goods and waste which require great efforts to manage. For young people they are important as a means of communication, of the identities they are busy creating.

Understood as communication, and the money used to buy them as a means to independence, the products of commercial culture should be much less frightening to us. Communication is momentary and personal and young people are quite capable of matching the strategies of companies which offer material for those moments. Anything can be sold, but how it is used is another matter.

In their study *Reflecting on youth arts*, Michael Wimmer and Ebrû Sonuç argue that the greater the importance of young people as consumers, the more they become a target group for commercial interests, and for the cultural industries in particular. They argue that young people are probably the main purchasers of the various products of the music industries ; they are the main cinemagoers and they are deeply interested in fashion and style. They agree that :

The cultural industries are not interested in young people just as purchasers and consumers, they value them as content producers. Cultural enterprises are greatly dependent on the creativity of young people, in the fields of music, design and computer programming. In an era of rapid changes in fashion and taste there is a constant need for new approaches. Often the style of a certain sub-culture, deliberately developed to clash with the commercial mainstream, is the basis of tomorrow's new mainstream. This circle is surely the most important way for young people to gain access to the world of the arts, passively and actively. But it is still necessary for political responsibility to be taken to guarantee that a great variety of arts activities is at the disposal of young people.

Roger Hill argues that for young people, the construction of identity is an active process which accepts, rejects and transforms what it finds. Young people approach commercial culture in this spirit.

And if commerce has laboured to create innumerable consumer tribes it has thus invented a major difficulty for itself, because these tribes are harder to control and manipulate than single youth market. And the sub-divided market does contain coherent patterns of taste and affiliation which insulate young people against pure exploitation. A tribe of " crusties ", living a new Age ethic, will be resistant to unnecessary consumption. Ravers will avoid clubs with poor-quality management. Fans of the latest boy- or girl-band may not buy music by anyone else.

Commerce and youth have an intense relationship. Commercial culture, far more than public programmes, matches the speed and rhythms of young people's lives. It tries to speak their language and to create a commercial " underground " to absorb their anarchic energies.

Most of all it would like to create and fix their language and patterns of consumption but it will always fail because, in this at least, it becomes institutional and meets the same sceptical detachment which young people apply to all institutions. It can never be more than a mirror of their lives, however much the battle for influence seems to rage to and from, and despite its economic need to represent them they will in the end represent themselves. We could say that the world's commerce is a more flexible, responsive thing for this spirited interaction with young people.

If commercial culture, from a young person's point of view, is about communication rather than commodity then the arts, according to Roger Hill, are about the " how " rather than the " what " of self-expression. If arts institutions accept this they can begin to draw upon the busy agenda of youth. The arts as social engineering will be abandoned – young people can detect a hidden agenda very easily. Artists can be left to pursue their own creative potential whilst the skilled enablers and facilitators of what is sometimes called " community arts " can assist in developing autonomous self-expression.

The neighbourhoods and districts of our settlements will be more important as the settings for creativity than individual institutions. The arts should expect to take their place within a much wider range of cultural expressions available to young people. Projects which address fundamental social needs, like the provision of housing or protection of the environment or achieving justice for a minority, and can use the arts to achieve this, will have the greatest power and influence. Traditions of community culture can be re-introduced to a young generation which runs the risk of losing that sense of continuity, a connection with their future via the past. The arts are not about creating audiences for themselves – the very idea of audiences has changed over the last two decades and will continue to evolve – but about finding a role for themselves in a busy, motivated world. If the arts do not fulfil a function in our growth and self-education, or assist in the processes of change in society, what claim do they have on our support ?

Interculturalism

All member states face the same cultural challenge : how to meet the growing complexities of cultural diversity while maintaining some sense of cultural cohesion. The terms used indicate often radically different assumptions and approaches. In some countries the key concept is " multiculturalism ". Jennifer Williams is concerned that this approach can reinforce differences and encourage separatism rather than integration. She prefers the term " interculturalism " to equal respect for all cultures. The intercultural approach has an ambitious aim : " to form a new open cultural identity which is not Eurocentric nor ethnocentric, nor is it passionately tied to any particular beliefs and values. Intercultural education allows for the emergence of new cultural forms linked to contemporary experience. "

> Those who recommend extending multicultural education or developing intercultural education usually agree that most curricula are biased towards the dominant culture. One way of obtaining real understanding and mutual tolerance between members of different communities is to cut back on existing cultural curricula and to include lessons on other cultures. By getting pupils to realise that there are other ways of thinking, they can learn that their own culture is not intrinsically superior nor others inferior.

New political and social solutions might form, based on new ethical and cognitive standpoints. For each country the starting point for intercultural provision for young people will depend on a number of factors :

• *History*

Is there a policy of assimilation, are there specific cultural policies in place which take into account differences in language, religious background, and/or cultural traditions ; are there forums for democratic discourse on matters of cultural provision ?

• *The pressure for change*

Are there pressing problems such as racial or social unrest ; is there a desire to increase audiences for and participation in established arts or to facilitate new forms of expression ; are there patterns of employment and training that address the situation for young people ?

• *Funding*

Do the government systems local, national and international have cultural policies and programmes aimed specifically at young people ; do any private sources such as foundations and/or businesses have them; do any funding sources have specific policies for encouraging intercultural understanding ?

The problems of cultural pluralism " cannot be minimised nor can they be solved by wishful thinking or moralising. Intercultural education is an active framework within which to work. "

26

IV. The needs of young people

Definitions of the arts are changing rapidly, not least through interaction with new technologies and popular culture. One of the most significant influences is the increasing impact of new technologies. Technology has always interacted closely with art practice. Artists in all disciplines use tools and materials : the tools and materials available not only facilitate arts practice but can change its very nature. The availability of oil paints and stretched canvas had a profound impact on the growth of European painting, as did the development of lens-based technologies on visual arts world wide. The new technologies, especially information technologies are bringing about a revolution in many areas of arts practice. They are also collapsing long-established distinctions between artists, technologists and scientists. The burgeoning field of multimedia is a key example of ways in which old discipline boundaries are breaking down in the face of new tides of creative innovation.

For the most part, arts and cultural policies are defined and evaluated by professionals who may be increasingly remote from young people's artistic and aesthetic interests and passions. Involving young people in the processes of policy development may hold many benefits for young people themselves and for the dynamism and creativity of cultural policies.

Aesthetic and creative activities have central roles in the lives of young people. Roger Hill argues that young people are artists in life, they specialise in the artistry of growth. Because their section of the life-line is so important their artistry is of a unique and special kind.

> It is particularly flexible and moves beyond the usual conventions of self-expression. Hungry for an exact expression of their situation in any moment young people select and discard a huge range of available materials, ideas, words and images with impressive speed. The past and other contemporary cultures provide them with the material to create an individual style which is a popular and practical version of the aesthetic we have come to call post-modern. Strangeness and difference, aspects of the Other, are particularly valuable to them in establishing the unique character which will guarantee their presence in the world. Young people also require flexibility of the things they take over. Their great skill is in transformation. They can make ordinary and mundane objects special with new uses and combinations. They adapt and they invent. Their language is precise, original and distinctive. They experiment with sensuality, the feel of substances, the pleasurable properties of material goods.

Young people make determined efforts to represent themselves, in response to pressures from outside to accept ready-made representation. Autonomy is important to them and this impulse has produced new developments and cultural potential. In response to changes in employment patterns self-employment has increased in many countries and in Europe many young people have set up their own businesses in expressive work of almost every kind. Willis notes that new forms of creativity result from this creative momentum, involving networking, exchanges and small-scale production, for example. Many of these are rooted in the use of new technologies. According to Roger Hill, these are further evidence of a singular impulse to independence in young people's artistry of life. He argues that young people come to new technology with relatively open minds and a great enthusiasm for mastery.

> We know of their skill and fascination for the systems and networks and also how much these systems are at the forefront of a battle between public and private control. For adult society this new frontier has generated unease – at the challenge to ideas of authorship and ownership, the threat to privacy, the spread of surveillance, the multiplication of information and manipulation of reality made possible with digital technology. If wealth is the passport to control of our destinies then media technology is where that wealth will be spent. Different areas of technology now seem about to merge. Biotechnology and genetic engineering will be seen to connect with information management in a comprehensive capability to re-order our destinies. We feel less and less able to trust anyone with that capability, yet corporations investing in technology are relying on younger and younger minds to make advances in the field. This is a major test of our capacity to entrust our future to a younger generation.

Young people's lives are in a state of transition. However much they may try to achieve a " finish or stability it would be wrong for this life-period of change and adjustment. At best they achieve a series of creative actions. The identity which they are creating is, if they are lucky, open-ended ". Roger Hill identifies the following elements which young people draw on " to incorporate a satisfying sense of self " :

Direct and indirect experience

Young people's lives are shaped by two categories of experience, that of the locality where they grew up and what happened to them there, vividly, personally and directly, and that of the wider world they may never know directly but will receive vast amounts of information about through a number of media, indirectly and suggestively. Both kinds of experience have a place in the growth of identity.

The personal and the global

Young people want to find a level of moral certainty in two particular areas, in their relations with others and in their response to world affairs. Although these may develop separately the growing identity needs both to be satisfying.

Attitude

The word is used independently – as in, " You've got attitude " –, to express a definite but flexible response to what is going on around the individual. It assumes a moral view even if this is not conventional or totally coherent. Without " attitude " identity has no points of connection with the world.

Idealism

The construction of identity is very engrossing and breeds a hard, instinctive realism, but is incomplete without the element of idealism whether this is a vision of the perfect place for the individual in the scheme of things or a developed idea of a better structured society.

A sense of uniqueness

Every young person strives to establish for themselves a sense of acting independently and autonomously, of being self-sufficient and able to reject imposed solutions to their problems, all of which will contribute to a feeling of distinctive identity.

Social acceptance

The principle which balances uniqueness is acceptance in which independence, autonomy and self-sufficiency all find a respectful relationship with the society within which the individual moves.

Security

An identity which leaves the individual exposed to high levels of criticism or comment will lead to personal unhappiness so the construction of identity incorporates protective elements which may not be truly representative of itself but which preserve it from too much outside influence while it continues to grow in independence.

Escape routes

As well as creating protective versions of the self the growing personality needs to be able to withdraw completely from engagement with the world from time to time. Young people choose cultural and social identities which allow for these periodic disappearances.

Feeling real

Reality is not an abstraction for young people, it is something they test on the senses. A moment in which identity has reached a satisfying coherence will be " real " in a very direct and sensual way, present and inclusive even if the growth it represents is more intellectual and completed.

A sense of freedom

Identity is formed in a continuous way and is satisfying to the extent that it feels open-ended with a number of options for further or alternative growth. This feeling is the essential " freedom " of youth.

Jennifer Williams argues that the arts are powerful vehicles for developing a sense of identity. If adults and institutions are to contribute constructively, they must understand the perspectives from which young people view them. She quotes the following lessons which, according to William Cleveland of the Center for the Study of Art and Community in the USA, all adults should learn and remember :

1. For young people today there are far fewer places where creative exploration and experimentation can be safely practised. Arts education is an endangered species. They need this desperately. Not because it would be nice, as a recreational alternative, but because it is their job to learn by exploring and questioning the world they were born into. We need this desperately. Not because it seems like the right pedagogical thing to do, but because, without this raw and exuberant feedback we have lost our only opportunity to

learn from and collaborate with the next generation on our future.

2. Young people want to be respected for the varied and unique voices they bring to the conversation taking place in their communities. They are particularly concerned about the conversations that take place that affect their lives but do not involve them. They will be heard eventually.

3. Young people do not themselves want to be subjects of faddish experiments, cultural or otherwise foisted upon them by the adult world.

4. Young artists want an artistic workplace that provides both form and freedom. They are, at once, attracted to the improvisation and the discipline inherent to the creative process.

5. Young people want us to be clear about what goes and doesn't go. As young artists and citizens they want to be informed of the rules. Where is it safe ? Where is there danger ?

6. Young people do not want to be romanticised. They want to be respected for their capacities and potentials. They want to be acknowledged and accepted for what they know and what they don't know.

7. Aspiring young artists want their artist/teacher/mentors to be honest and very clear about what they know and don't know. They can recognise, and are insulted by fakery. They

want the adults working with them to have their stuff to-gether.

8. When the adult world brings the power and force of the creative process into their lives young people do not want a one night stand. They do not want to be turned on and left behind.

9. Once a commitment has been made, young people want regularity, dependability, and commitment from the artists who become a part of their lives.

10. As they get older and more invested in creative relation-ships young people want to be given opportunities to gain some degree of ownership of the process and outcome of the work.

11. Young people want to make and do more than they want to be told about, talk about, or analyse what is going on.

12. Young people want to know how their art making can contribute to the needs of their peers and their communities.

13. Young people want to be held to high standards. They know when they are being subjected to the tyranny of low expectations.

14. Young people want to know what you think about their work. They want you to be fair and honest.

15. Young people would like adults to respect their cultural practices without dominating, appropriating, or romanticising them.

16. Young people want their artist/teacher/mentors to take care of themselves. They don't want burned out teachers delivering half-baked programs.

17. Young people want to celebrate.

18. Young people want you to lighten up.

19. Young people sometimes want you to listen and not offer advice.

20. Young people want to eat and dance and make music.

21. Young people want to love and be loved.

Against this background, what actions are needed, and in what areas of work ?

V. The current provision

The arts in schools

There is a pressing need to evaluate the quality of arts teaching in formal education, and for curriculum development. An initial survey of the arts in formal education in member states was conducted in the preliminary phase of the " Culture, Creativity and the Young " project. This provided valuable information on structures of provision for the arts in formal education in schools. It confirmed that existing patterns of provision for the arts in schools vary considerably between member states. An important factor is the extent to which the school curriculum in general is specified centrally. In some countries, there are strict prescriptions in content and assessment criteria to be followed by schools and teachers in all subjects. In others, there is freedom within national frameworks for schools and teachers to develop their own curricular content and teaching methods. In some countries, the arts are given a positive profile in national policy statements and schools are strongly encouraged to develop them both within and outside the formal curriculum. In general terms, this is not the case.

All policy statements on national education routinely emphasise the importance of the cultural dimension, and of promoting creative abilities. The necessity of engaging children in the practice and study of the arts is also emphasised. In practice, as the patterns of provision in the national profiles indicate, the actual status of and provision for the arts is less prominent. For the most part, the main disciplines taught are art and music. In the majority of national systems, they are compulsory in primary education and for the first two or three years of secondary education. Beyond that point they, almost universally, become optional. In all cases, the arts have a lower status than mathematics and science.

In all countries, significant processes of reform are in hand in the substance and the management of educational systems. In some, serious attempts are being made to re-evaluate the place and significance of the arts, and in particular the relations of children, teachers and artists. There is a need for further information and debate on the content, style and quality of arts teaching in schools, and on its perceived value and effects for young people themselves.

The roles of the arts in education

The aims of education, as summarised in the various national profiles, identify a number of different areas of achievement. The arts are related, with different emphases, to each of them. They include :

Intellectual development

The arts are among the ways that human beings organise their understanding of experience and provide vivid examples of this diversity of intelligence. The musician, dancer, or visual artist is working in specific modes of conception : they are having and expressing visual, aural or kinaesthetic ideas. One of the key roles of arts education is to contribute to the full development of each individual's intellectual capacities.

Emotional development

Feelings and emotions are forms of evaluations. Grief at a death, elation at a birth, the pleasure of success – are part of individuals' perceptions of these events and express the values they attach to them. For the most part young people's feelings and the roles of feeling in intellectual, personal and social development are not taken into account in education. All curriculum work may affect the pupil's view of the world and his or her life of feeling. Work in the arts has particular importance in giving status and a positive place to personal feelings and values, in enabling a direct consideration of values and feelings, and in giving forms to feeling.

Cultural development

Human cultures consist of the values, beliefs, codes and conventions of behaviour that emerge through our relationships with others, and they vary hugely from place to place and from time to time. The arts are among the ways on which different cultural values are forged and reinforced through shared expression. They are among the ways in which young people can learn about and reflect upon the cultural influences on their own lives ; and in which they can participate in the formation and reformation of cultural values.

Moral development

The arts are deeply concerned with questions of value. No teacher can go far into the education of feelings without encountering questions of value, of social morality and of moral education. The arts can offer positive and immediate ways of raising questions of value and of exploring the cultural perceptions to which they relate.

Aesthetic development

Arts education is concerned with deepening young people's sensitivities to the formal qualities – and the pleasures and meanings – of the arts and, through this process, with extending the range and depth of their aesthetic sensibilities and judgement. Arts education is concerned with enabling young people to make informed and increasingly discriminating judgements about their own and other people's work in the arts.

Creative development

Industry and commerce want those entering employment to show powers of innovation, initiative and application in solving problems and pursuing opportunities. These are widely held to be pre-requisites for economic health. For the growing numbers of those for whom conventional employment is ceasing to be an option, these powers will be essential. Creative thought and action should be fostered in all areas of education : in the arts they are central.

Physical and perceptual development

Arts education involves the development of many different kinds of skill. These include the technical skills that young people acquire in controlling different media of expression, the perceptual skills of observation, composition and evaluation, and the language skills in talking and writing about work. The arts also call on a wide range of social skills which are vital to the collaborative work needed in many arts projects. In these and other respects the arts contribute in significant ways to personal and social education.

Personal and social development

The arts provide all pupils with the opportunities to explore a fuller range of their abilities, and some pupils with the chance to discover for the first time where their real abilities lie. The experience of success in achievement, and enjoyment in learning which the arts demonstrably promote can raise immeasurably the self-esteem of young people and their estimation of their own abilities, and greatly increase their motivation for learning across the curriculum.

These objectives are central to the forms of education that are needed if European states are to respond adequately to the challenges they face, and to keep pace with the processes of co-operative development to which, to varying degrees, they are becoming committed. The need for improved provision for the arts in education is not limited to schools. As Jennifer Williams notes, the wide acceptance of the concept of lifelong learning has helped to generate opportunities for creative work in both formal and informal settings including special settings such as prisons, play groups, old people's home and hospitals. It has also helped to develop thinking about new uses of facilities such as the playground and the school library during out-of-school hours. The potential benefits of sustained arts provision in all such settings are summarised by one study (McLaughlin, 1990) :

• The arts enhance students' creativity and increase creative thinking and problem solving ability.

• The arts are an integral part of human development in dimensions such as the use of both hemispheres of the brain ; development of the cognitive, affective and psychomotor skills ; and of individual learning styles.

• The arts increase communication skills vitally needed in today's complex society with its emphasis on technology and mass communication.

• The arts enhance basic literacy skills (literacy here being defined more broadly than just fundamental reading skills) to include cultural literacy and literacy of non-verbal stimuli.

• The arts enable students to acquire aesthetic judgement, a skill which enhances daily life and affects individual choices as well as group decisions concerning the human environment.

• The arts develop self-esteem and help students to gain a more positive self-concept. Low self-esteem is at the root of major societal problems such as violence, teenage suicide, and substance abuse.

• The arts provide students with better cross-cultural understanding through knowledge of civilisations and cultures past and present. In terms of human relationships, failure to understand the pluralistic nature of society often leads to racial, class and ethnic tensions.

• The arts enhance the school atmosphere and can help improve student attendance and decrease the dropout rate.

• The arts provide numerous career opportunities both in the commercial/entertainment industry and in the non-profit sector.

• The arts improve student performance in other subject areas.

• The arts are a valuable teaching tool in working with special populations such as students with physical or mental disabilities, those with limited local language proficiency or the economically disadvantaged.

Culture and the community

The arts are not a separate area of a community's life : they are a pervasive dimension of it. If language is the heart of cultural identity, it tends to beat most quickly in its literary and poetic traditions. If religion is one of the main repositories of a culture's moral values, the experiences it speaks to tend to be most deeply expressed in music, art and dance. The history of society is not only constituted by political and economic events, but by the lived experience of its members within a dynamic social culture. This lived experience of other times is often best evoked through the music, art and poetry of the day in which it was given contemporary form and meaning. For these reasons, arts education – making and learning about the arts – has a central role to play in cultural and in intercultural education ; that is, one which :

a. helps young people to understand cultural diversity : by bringing them into contact with cultural values, conventions and ideologies that vary from their own ;

b. acknowledges cultural relativity : by helping them to clarify and compare their own with other values and attitudes ;

c. helps them to understand the evolutionary nature of culture and the processes of cultural change : by relating contemporary ideologies to historical circumstances and developments from which they have emerged.

Jennifer Williams argues that the principal motivation for young people's involvement in arts activities is communication. As well as being enjoyable, arts practice offers many opportunities to communicate, to discover expressive ability, to gain social skills and for enjoyment. Many reports on youth arts argue the positive benefits of involvement in the arts, but do not use the word education. Results are usually expressed in terms of skills gained or personal development. Young people are motivated by fun, a chance to express themselves and by what their friends are interested in doing.

Working with artists

In many countries, professional artists work outside the conventional settings of theatres, galleries and concert halls in a wide range of community and social projects. These developments have important implications for how the arts are perceived :

By taking art out of the gallery and theatre and into other environments, artists were creating a new context for the reception of an artwork and questioning the purpose of art. This is an important point : the social/community-based nature of this kind of work has often meant that it gets characterised as some kind of social service with the artistic element existing as little more than a mechanism through which this service is delivered. The real picture is rather more complex, however, and certainly more interesting. What these programmes and individuals are advocating is clearly not " art for art's sake " – yet neither is it art as therapy or as social service. The artists who work in other places are arguing for an art that truly engages with human experience – having positive implications for both the art form and for those individuals and communities involved in its making. (Phillips, 1997)

Jennifer Williams comments that control of arts institutions has often been in the hands of a dominant cultural group with policies reflecting their own interests and traditions. Power and resources are difficult to relinquish. A number of attempts have been made to redress the balance in favour of a wider proportion of the population. In the United Kingdom, the Arts Council of Great Britain developed an ethnic minorities action plan in the 1980s. This helped to raise the profile of the arts of minority groups, especially among subsidised arts organisations – but without going far enough to satisfy the perceived needs and demands of minority artists and audiences. The Sami people, indigenous people living across Norway, Finland, Sweden and Russia, have received state funding for a Language Council, Educational Council and Trade Council as well as for a theatre group, library and radio station. *(In from the margins, 1997)*

A number of projects and centres in Europe collaborate in the provision of non-European arts and provide models of initiatives contributing to a stable pluralist environment. A few, new style organisations exist which avoid the trap of turning non-European contemporary art into an exotic footnote to the European mainstream, by presenting work from a plurality of world cultures according to an equal exchange and representation of artists previously excluded from the cultural canon. A good example of this kind of institution is the Institute of International Visual Arts (inIVA) in London, which gives priority to visual arts practice and scholarship of the highest quality which have not been adequately represented or disseminated.

Many schools have programmes which place artists in the classroom, to demonstrate their art form and to perform. The presence of artists, if well prepared for, can enrich teaching and the climate of the school as a whole. The Elia's study– *Working with young people* – identifies the following main benefits in such schemes.

The benefits for young people *include opportunities to :*

• gain an insight into the professional arts world ;
• understand the artistic process ;
• try out new approaches ;
• develop artistic skills ;
• gain and display enthusiasm, enjoyment and confidence ;
• identify with the positive role models that artists can provide ;
• develop positive work relationships.

The benefits for artists *include opportunities to :*

• reach a wider audience ;
• work with others ;
• help others to develop their abilities.

46

The benefits for group leaders *(including* teachers *in schools)*
include opportunities to :

• observe another adult working with the group (or class) ;
• develop their own interest in the arts ;
• deal with personal and social issues ;
• develop closer relationships with the young people and
other staff ;
• involve the wider community (including parents) ;
• make links with other groups (or schools) ;
• promote a positive image of the group (or school).

In schools, the benefits for teachers *also include opportunities
to :*

• contribute to the arts curriculum ;
• contribute to the arts curriculum for pupils and students
with special needs ;
• enrich the curriculum overall.

Artists can be enormously powerful ambassadors for intercultural understanding as well as act as positive role models.
The benefits are not automatic. There are several reasons for
this.

• Teachers are not trained to work with professionals from
others fields.

• Scheduling of participation in arts activities can be difficult,
as can negotiating differences in educational approaches and
content.

• Financing partnerships can be complicated as many arts funding systems are primarily interested in supporting projects that are initiated by professional artists or arts institutions. They are often less ready to support projects submitted directly by the schools.

• Education budgets can be inflexible, especially when it comes to spending commitments other than school facilities.

Artists are not always prepared to apply their work to teaching. As the Elia study notes :

> It would be true to say that, with respect to the professional development of artists, existing arts education and training programmes tend to concentrate on the nurturing of their individual voices with lesser attention given to the changing role of artists in an increasingly complex and sophisticated environment. There is a need for artists to be skilled in other areas – in particular teaching and instructing/facilitating, since high percentages of professional artists (from all artforms) have some experience of " passing on " the skills they have developed in an education or training context.
>
> However, there is very little specific training for artists who wish (or are invited) to work in schools. Most artists receive their training at a specialist art training institution, or through a specialist course at a university or college. Few of these institutions or courses provide training in the skills required to work in schools.

Many people in the arts world – administrators, programmers and artists – have some way to go before they can collaborate comfortably with other sectors. This problem stems in part from the training which leads them to believe that their skills and insights are somehow better than those of other partners. Many arts professionals need to realise that people working in education know a good deal about the nature of learning and also have something unique to bring to the collaboration.

Michael Wimmer and Ebrû Sonuç identify the same difficulties and propose some solutions :

> At the moment most teachers specialise in particular subjects, and are not always prepared to act in teams to support multi-subject projects or to co-operate with external cultural institutions or initiatives. During their professional training they are not usually required to consider the significance of the arts for education nor contemporary methods of dealing with the arts during learning processes.
>
> The future professional role of all teachers has to encompass not only some knowledge, but also an ability to make use of the arts and artists whenever possible in school.
>
> Even specialist arts teachers are not always used to working with artists. Most of the time spent on these subjects (where they are offered at all) is devoted to the history of the arts, especially the history of music, the visual arts and selected aspects of literature. The presentation often stops around the beginning of the 20th century, which means that most pupils have no experience of contemporary art forms and their representatives at school.
>
> The rest of the time pupils are asked to do practical work to develop their own creativity. Most of this practical work, meant to compensate for the one-sided dominance of knowledge acquisition in other subjects, has nothing to do

with the real life of the pupils and results in the opposite of creativity.

Co-operation with artists could play a rather innovative role, offering unconventional points of view, but also providing new instruments for dealing with the complexity of today's social reality. In these circumstances the artist cannot simply replace the classroom teacher. Both have to find new roles : the teacher as moderator of the shared learning process, and the artist as an expert in aesthetics working together with the teacher and the young people.

When implementing these new forms of co-operation, it has to be borne in mind that for many teachers the arts world is strange, even dangerous, and the opposite of constricting rules of the normal school system. On the other hand, many artists also nurture some prejudice against the school system, remembering their own (often bad) experience when they were pupils themselves, and not being aware of any current developments in schools.

Common training programmes could help. Such training would provide the opportunity to become more closely acquainted with each other's professional backgrounds, and make possible the development of new forms of co-operation.

In each school there should be at least one teacher as a " multiplier " and co-ordinator of cultural and art-specific activities. During their special training programmes, project-orientation, team-building, co-operation with artists and cultural institutions, evaluation, public relations and fund-raising should be covered. Cultural co-ordinators should establish a network, and therefore have regular contacts at least at local and regional level, to share their experience and to develop further common activities.

Social welfare and health

There is a growing sense among social and health practitioners that the arts can enable young people to develop personally and socially and provide them with skills for employment. Artists and children together can develop ways of expressing issues which complement the more clinical approaches. The arts can be applied with equal effect in therapeutic settings. For instance, the use of story telling and theatre with young people to explore issues of personal or social concern. The arts are also used increasingly in initiatives to alert young people to the dangers of HIV, drug abuse or gang violence.

Although there are such collaborations, they are not a major feature in the policy of either the social or health sectors. There is no protocol for who should pay for these cooperations : there is also much to be done to combine the best features of these different sectors without compromising the effects of either. The Finnish National Research and Development Centre for Health and Welfare dedicated its annual conference in 1997 for health and social workers to the culture of social and health work. The programme included a well-attended two day seminar on the social application and impact of the arts. Through such an intensive concentrated look at examples of practice, evaluation techniques and outcomes, the workers had a much clearer picture of the arts as a possible resource and partner in their work. It is only after this kind of visionary discussion that collaborations on any significant scale can be formulated.[5]

Cultural institutions

One of the most significant developments in the mainstream arts world is the huge growth of education as an accepted function of arts institutions. Practically every cultural institution in Europe has, or is planning to have, an education programme. Even those which do not have their own programmes are often used by educators as educational resources. These programmes are developing in many different directions including work created for schools, for older people and for young people. They are enabling orchestras, theatres, museums and other organisations to develop new relationships with audiences and with potential participants. Michael Wimmer and Ebrû Sonuç emphasise the importance of these initiatives :

> In almost all European countries there is an impressive number of cultural and artistic institutions, such as museums, galleries, theatre companies, orchestras, archives, libraries and publishing houses, film institutions, urban cultural centres or rural cultural initiatives. Often these have a long tradition, enabling them to develop their highly professional roles in their respective fields.

> But many of these institutions are not only acknowledged within a highly specialised circle. They also cater for a broader public and provide educational activities for several less specialised target groups, including young people. In this context a new profession has been created, that of " education officer " responsible for mutual productive relations with users and audiences. These education officers are in charge of arrangements for current programmes, but also have to establish the special needs and expectations of the different target groups for consideration in further programming.

For many members of artistic staffs of these institutions, it is quite natural to work with young people in and outside schools : musicians and composers take part in different music education programmes ; actors work together with pupils in drama workshops ; film-makers give advice on how to produce a semi-professional video ; others help to organise an interdisciplinary performance. The young people have the opportunity not only to become acquainted with some artists, but also to look backstage and gain an idea of the complex and professional nature of such cultural institutions. Sometimes it is possible for young people to use the institutions' equipment on their own and to present the results of their arts venture to a broader public.

Looking at some public, but also some private, funding procedures the educational aspect seems to be increasingly important. This very obviously legitimises the donation of public and private money for artistic activities. The English Arts Council now spends about 80 % of its funding on cultural institutions which are prepared to offer educational activities. In the Scandinavian countries and the Netherlands, too, cultural policy programmes are moving in the same direction, while in other cultural centres such as Austria, political and administrative decision-makers are still at the very beginning.

Some institutions, especially in the field of music, are also trying to establish international forms of co-operation.

" Unfortunately, beyond naming education as a priority, many arts institutions have not yet clarified the real educational purposes of these programmes nor how education programmes relate to artistic policies. Is education for building bigger audiences, more informed audiences ? Are the resources being used as a starting point for the development of the creative powers of the individual, or for growing community understanding ? " (Williams, 1995)

If an education programme is designed specifically to attract more people into the institution, it is important to understand what deters people in the first place. A survey in England suggested that social class is one important factor : educational disadvantage another. Poverty can exclude some groups. The survey's statistical evidence also showed that the use of museums by ethnic minorities was low. People with disabilities are inhibited by poor access.

Through education programmes, cultural institutions have the greatest potential for promoting intercultural understanding. Most institutions have an open policy, inviting all schools to participate in the programmes they offer. Consequently many institutions work with people from a variety of cultural backgrounds. If the programme leaders are sensitive to issues of cultural pluralism they will take these differences into account and design programmes accordingly. Nonetheless, cultural institutions can be unprepared for work with children from differing cultural backgrounds. The basic material, the arts collection or theatre work, often comes from a single culture or tradition and may not speak directly to young people from different backgrounds. There can be problems with the staff responsible for outreach or education, particularly if they have not been trained specifically for this work.

Well-structured programmes can provide powerful ways of promoting intercultural understanding. Programme leaders and participating artists can be important role models for the young people taking part. If the policy exists only within the education programme and not in the overall artistic policies of the institution, the benefits are mitigated.[6] For Michael Wimmer and Ebrû Sonuç this points to the vital need to improve liaison and mediation between the arts and education sectors.

> While many schools have developed their cultural profile, and many cultural institutions their educational profile, there is an increasing need for appropriate mediation between the two sectors. Schools wishing to step up their cultural activities can benefit from a service offering them specific know-how. And cultural institutions wishing to develop their educational programmes or to work together with schools or other educational institutions can sometimes take advantage of certain services.

> This is why the Austrian government decided – as much as twenty years ago – to establish an organisation called the Austrian Cultural Service (Österreichischer Kultur-Service, ÖKS) which is responsible for providing information, service and also funding for arts and education programmes. ÖKS, with its specific profile as an " arm's-length " organisation responsible to the Ministry of Education and Cultural Affairs, seems to be more or less unique in Europe. Its main objective is to improve theoretical as well as practical aspects of arts and education, i.e. to find appropriate forms of co-operation for teachers, artists and other representatives of cultural institutions.

> In other European countries these tasks are fulfilled by institutions with different profiles, such as the Netherlands Institute of Arts Education (LOKV), which is responsible for improving arts education programmes in and outside state schools, the Arts Councils in the United Kingdom, with separate arts education departments, and various Swedish organisations which run

programmes to help arrange exhibitions and concert and theatre performances throughout the country. In France, some of
these tasks are carried out within the Ministry of Culture, while
others are shared among several ministries.

Developing networks

There is a wide range of work now going on across member
states in providing for the creative and cultural development
of young people. The pattern is not even, between disciplines, fields of work or between countries and regions. An
important role is played by the international networking organisations which exist to bring practitioners into contact
and to promote information and good practice across national and sectoral boundaries. There is a growing number of
such networks which specialise in linking youth initiatives in
the arts and cultural arenas.[7] The training, contacts, good
ideas and support available to members through networks
are a vital catalyst to their evolution. Networks are not easy
to maintain and require a great deal of time and energy.
Funding can also be a problem. Some support has been
found from private foundations and/or government depart-
ments that believe in investing in youth programmes and
also understand how network services can strengthen the
work of the local providers.

Both ethnic-specific and non-ethnic specific organisations
benefit from networks and from collaborations. The links
that are made among participants bring access to targeted
markets, contacts within those markets for bookings, press
coverage and in some cases non-arts related funding

sources. Some sources for funds are more interested in the market served than the programme offered.

The need for training

The Elia study confirms that there is a need to give higher priority in member states to the arts in the training of teachers and to education and community action in the training of artists. The arts are concerned with the qualities of experience : and the quality of arts experience is a key factor in cultural policy and development. Too often, the training of teachers takes little account of the need to promote the creative and cultural development of young people. Equally, the training of artists often includes little or no consideration of the wider social and community roles they can fulfil during their own creative lives. There is a need for a careful review of the training of artists and teachers, as key agents in cultural change and development. Most teachers, especially for secondary schools, have been trained to teach particular subjects in particular ways. Teachers have not always been trained to innovate. Faced with increasing cultural diversity in their classrooms and in the community, teachers are reflecting on strategies to enable young people to reach their full capacity and obtain some degree of intercultural understanding. The Elia study draws the following general conclusions :

• provision for the training of teachers in the arts in schools is extensive, and further more detailed work would need to be done to ascertain the quality and effectiveness of such training ;

• opportunities for young people in " traditional " extra-curricular arts activities or activities outside the school would appear to be limited to certain art form areas, and it is not clear whether this is the same throughout Europe ;

• provision for the training of teachers and those working with young people in " traditional " extra-curricular arts activities or activities outside the school requires further more detailed work to ascertain the extent, quality and effectiveness of such training ;

• opportunities for artists to work in schools would appear to be increasing across Europe ;

• provision for the training of artists in schools is beginning to emerge, although the breadth of such training is confusing and the developments are generally ad hoc – they encompass :

– training (as an " extra " added to an art form course or qualification) in certain skill areas to enable individual artists to work in a school environment ;

– training (as an " extra " added to an art form course or qualification) in certain skill areas to enable artists to work as part of a group or company which targets schools for performances, visits or workshops ;

– greater opportunities for artists and art workers to work in non-traditional environments are also emerging – there are increasing examples of projects and activities where artists and arts workers are becoming involved with young people in non-traditional environments – working with youth groups, in health-related environments and issues, in a community setting, and in other more specific situations (e.g. prisons) ;

• provision for the training of artists and arts workers to work in non-traditional environments is extremely limited, with a few opportunities in areas such as the following :

– training (as an " extra " added to an art form course or qualification) in certain skill areas to enable individual artists to work in a non-traditional environment ;

– training (as an " extra " added to an art form course or qualification) in certain skill areas to enable artists to work as part of a group or company which targets non-traditional environments for performances, visits or workshops ;

– a small number of specialised courses which provide individuals (who may or may not be artists) with certain specific skills to work in non-traditional environments (" community arts " courses) ;

• the range of skills identified in this report as being relevant to artists and arts workers who work in schools and non-traditional environments would benefit from further consultation on a pan-European basis, although the authors are confident they represent an accurate initial summary of the relevant skills and knowledge ;

• it is likely that more opportunities will become available for artists and arts workers to work in schools and in non-traditional environments ;

• it is also likely that more artists will seek to take up these opportunities, as it would appear unlikely that the range of employment opportunities in traditional arts organisations and occupations is likely to increase in the foreseeable future – in fact, it is more than likely to decrease ;

• it would appear (although further more detailed research is necessary to confirm this) that current training provision for artists does not, in most cases, encompass training in the skills identified in this report as being relevant to work in schools and in non-traditional environments ;

• there would therefore appear to be an argument that providers of training for artists and arts workers need to examine their curriculum and consider the incorporation of training in the skill areas identified in this report to enable their graduates to have a fully rounded set of skills to address the broadest possible range of future employment opportunities.

Policy development

The study by Michael Wimmer and Ebrû Sonuç confirms the pressing need to develop national cultural policies, and categories of funding, which recognise the necessity of engaging young people in cultural programmes. Cultural policies and arts funding structures do not always make specific provision for the cultural development of young people. Existing policies often concentrate on the work of professional artists, on traditional definitions of the arts and on work with and by adults. Young people are engaged in a wide range of cultural and creative activities which often fall outside conventional definitions of the arts, and outside conventional categories of support. Michael Wimmer and Ebrû Sonuç call for more creative thinking by governments in the area of funding.

The tasks of the state have changed considerably in recent years. Political and economic changes have led to a considerable withdrawal by the state, not only in the east European countries, but also in the west. This has also had some repercussions for relations between the state, the arts and young people. It used to be a clear task of the state to convey certain cultural values and the most important forms of artistic expression to young people, helping them to find their place in society. The increasing diversity of life in society makes it difficult for the state authorities to decide which kind of culture should be conveyed, and which not.

Together with severe problems in maintaining public budgets, this political uncertainty also leads to shortages in cultural provision for young people. More and more it is the commercial sector which fills this vacuum. But, every crisis can also be regarded as an opportunity. At the same time the cultural and media industries are increasingly looking for young people who can contribute creativity and an unconventional expressiveness developed by working in the arts. Especially for these young people, who are in principle prepared top take some risks to develop their own future jobs in the cultural field, appropriate labour market policy measures are urgently needed.

Perhaps we also have to learn to be creative ourselves to develop new funding and resources. Up to now a lot of thinking has been done in the old way, according to which the state alone is responsible for the arts and for education. But other potential partners are also often systematically neglected. These partners may be private businesses, which of course are pursuing certain interests which have to be taken into account when negiotiating new forms of co-operation. As we are often stuck in our categories, carefully defending our own playground and unwilling to be disturbed, we do not take the opportunity to co-operate with other initiatives or institutions in the field, with whom a certain amount of synergy could be achieved.

At state level, further opportunities should be considered. We are concentrating far too much on the traditional. But it may no longer be exclusively the cultural or educational which is prepared to support youth arts activities. It may also be the social, tourism, transport or economic department, representatives of which understand the importance of the initiative.

Provision for youth arts can be made in a variety of funding categories such as addressing unemployment, building opportunities for special needs populations, working to ease civil unrest and others which will link work on the problems and challenges in the community or in various social settings with the participation of young people in the arts. Equally, they can be specific about, say, the training needs of targeted minority artists in arts administration or presentation skills. Usually funding programmes are open to application by groups meeting selective criteria.

The influence of the funding bodies on the direction and content of programming should not be underestimated. The language used in the guidelines for seeking funding and in the criteria for selection often becomes the primary planning language. For example, funding-led developments are responsible directly or indirectly for the amount of emphasis on intercultural understanding as a goal. If foundations or other funding bodies are highly motivated to encourage youth work that promotes intercultural understanding, there is a stronger likelihood that projects will follow this lead. Roger Hill identifies a number of key questions to inform policy-making :

We can ask the following questions of particular youth cultural activities whether they are individual or communal, public, private or commercial, institutional or otherwise.

Do these activities encompass a wide range of self-expression ?

Are the cultural forms involved predominantly flexible, original and experimental, or fixed, conventional and orthodox ?

Do the young people involved have control over the processes they are involved in and can they make effective decisions about their development ?

Has every effort been made to encourage an element of democracy in the organisation of the activities ?

Are the circumstances in which the activities take place sufficiently conducive to a free exercise of imagination and creative play ?

Do the activities benefit from an abundance of stimulus and resources ?

Does the structure of the activities, their innate patterning, reflect the texture and dynamic of the young participants' lives ?

Do the activities contribute to the young people's self-possession and a firm purchase upon the continuity of their lives ?

Do the activities, or the young people through the activities, engage with the larger issues of negotiating a place in society ?

Are any interventionist elements productive of, and conducive to, positive growth in society as a whole ?

Good policy documents set out a flexible framework on which to build towards particular goals. They are written to send signals to a wide network of providers and planners. There is no doubt that the more central a policy is in a community, the more likely that organisations will implement projects that follow that lead. Not only are people given a language with which to think about a particular subject – a clearly articulated policy can also generate a new climate of opportunity for the creative and cultural development of all young people.[8]

VI. The recommendations

The four thematic studies make a wide range of recommendations. They are encapsulated in the following key proposals which conclude the study by Jennifer Williams.

1. Youth programmes and policies in Europe should be integrated into all existing and future plans for creative cities, learning cities and working cities programmes.

2. Models of good practice that reflect the needs of young disabled people to have access to the arts should be documented and distributed to help in the formulation and implementation of youth policies.

3. The benefits of informal out-of-school centres for young people should be evaluated, including drop-in centres, after school clubs, music and video recording studios, and new technology centres.

4. The place of the arts and culture should be studied and recognised as a contributor to the social development of individuals.

5. The arts in the curriculum should be given more central support by school authorities.

6. Artists and arts experts should become more involved in the planning of both formal and informal education.

7. Existing cultural indicators should be refined to include a more specific focus on the long-term effects on young people of participation in and study of the arts.

8. Intercultural youth forums should be encouraged on the Internet and elsewhere.

9. Anti-racist training should be encouraged in connection with cultural provision for young people.

10. Cultural institutions should develop youth provision policies and programmes with specific intercultural goals, including opening main stream art forms and institutions to non-European artists and audiences.

11. Funds for young minority artists and arts institutions should be made available through specially targeted programmes.

12. Member states should develop a central cultural service for young people to prepare them for taking full part in the adult arts and cultural world.

Roger Hill concludes that two main themes emerge from his study. First, institutions must expect to become less institutional to absorb the impact of young people's creative growth, but that this is not only a relaxation of the basic structures, it is also a readiness to evolve. Second, institutions fulfil the function of a kind of " other " : interaction, sometimes conflict, with them helps young people to know better who they need to be. This is a role all institutions need to play with confidence and intelligence, remaining true to their essential nature but benefiting from the new flexibility this requires. According to Roger Hill, a society divided against itself will inflict damage on its young people.

> Despite enlightened policies and the United Nations Convention on the Rights of the Child they are still the victims of our contradictions. We have two major responsibilities in the present and the future : we must begin to honour young people for the uniqueness of their capabilities and the special value of their life-perspective ; we must also work to repair the damage done by our neglect of them.

If the shift in attitude will be difficult, the benefits will be immense.

Notes

[1] In 1988, the European Council adopted a resolution on the European Dimension in education, the purposes of which included :

> (...) to improve their [pupils] knowledge of the community and its member states in their historical, cultural, economic and social aspects and bring home to them the significance of the co-operation of the member states of the European community with other countries of Europe and the world.

The Maastricht Treaty provided for the explicit adoption of the European dimension in school curricula, in all appropriate European disciplines, for example, literature, languages, history, geography, social sciences, economics and the arts. The Council of Europe has emphasised the necessity for European development of intercultural education, one which promotes an active process of communication and interaction between cultures to the mutual enrichment of each. For these and other reasons, the European Dimension is now being promoted to varying degrees in many subjects in state school systems.

[2] See also the report of the European Round Table on " Human rights and cultural policies in a changing Europe – The right to participate in cultural life " held in Helsinki (Finland) from 30 April to 2 May 1993 and organised by Circle and the International Movement of Rights and Humanity, in co-operation with the Council of Europe. Circle publication No. 6, published by the Arts Council of Finland (Helsinki, 1994).

[3] This is the conception of culture that has underpinned the initiatives and inquiries of the report of the World Commission on Culture and Development *Our creative diversity* (1996) and which frames the growing field of cultural studies in universities world-wide.

[4] Michael Wimmer and Ebrû Sonuç note that the Anglo-American concept of the arts seems to be more open, whereas in the German version, for example, " Kunst " is still seen as the expression of a sophisticated and elabo-

rate artistic profession only to be understood and appreciated by educated people with appropriate experience. More than that, " Kunst " is still associated with fine arts, omitting the rest of artistic production, from literature, music, dance, architecture and all other visual art forms including the new media.

[5] An interesting series of experiments is being conducted in Ireland, which has the highest rate of long term unemployment in OECD countries. The project, designed and carried out by CAFE (Creative Activity for Everyone) on behalf of the Department of Arts, Culture and the Gaeltacht is described as a community intervention programme. It aims to establish the effect of widening arts awareness among the long term unemployed, including many young people. The aim is to explore the potential of cultural actions in addressing wider issues of social and vocational exclusion.

[6] A theatre which is committed to making its repertoire more representative of its community might create an intercultural youth group which could explore and develop local skills in acting and production. An example is the Theatre Royal Stratford East in London which has a cross-cultural policy including colour blind casting which takes no account of racial background and allows a rich ethnic representation in all productions.

[7] Michael Wimmer and Ebrû Sonuç identify the following key networks :

- The Elia (European League of Institutes of the Arts) is a European network of arts institutions. In 1996 Elia was asked by the European Commission to run the Arts Education Thematic Network established within the Commission's Socrates education programme. The main task of the Thematic Network is to conduct research into the current situation in the arts field in higher education in Europe.

- The EU Net Art (European Network of Arts Organisations for Children and Young People) is a network of over sixty organisations from twenty-one European countries in every artistic discipline. Its main task is to create more room for arts activities for children and young people in Europe. The following aims are also set: promoting opportunities for children and young people in Europe to experience the arts and to develop their own creativity, promoting art activities for children and young people as an important way of bringing adults and children together in the process of social learning, encouraging artistic and social encounters between artists and children and young people, facilitating the exchange of ideas and experience between art professionals in Europe who work for children and young people and assisting their collaborative ventures, promoting political awareness of the arts for children and young people in Europe and its importance to the next generation.

- The Efah (European Forum for the Arts & Heritage) is a forum for the arts and heritage organisations, associations and networks across Europe. Efah is committed to the following objectives: identifying and highlighting the needs or Europe's artistic community to European decision-makers and participating in the decision-making procedure, improving the exchange of information on the arts and heritage in Europe between the cultural sector and those involved in cultural policy-making, and acting as consultants in the field of arts and heritage to European, national and regional policy and decision-making bodies.

- There are also some art-specific networks, like Jeunesses Musicales or Assitej (International Association of Theatre for Children and Young People), operating as mediators in the field of music and theatre for young people. Assitej, an organisation associated with Unesco, is represented on every continent through fifty-six national sections.

[8] One such policy document is that of the Norwegian Department of Education. It very clearly and specifically states the ways that a good education can contribute to the spiritual, creative and social development of people, as well as articulating how individuals can become well rounded in their attitudes towards work, community service and the environment. Another document which might be called a policy support statement has been designed to help take ownership of the concepts and build towards solutions of their own. Published by the Scottish Consultative Council on Curriculum, *The heart of the matter* was circulated to more than 12 000 teachers in formal and informal education in Scotland. The document was written in connection with a new policy direction in curriculum terms which concerned the social development of young people. As the title implies it explores the basics of what contributes to the education of the person as a whole.

References

In from the margins: contribution to the debate on culture and development in Europe (1997), Council of Europe, Strasbourg.

Dupuis, X. (1995) " From the cultural dimension of development to the roles of the arts and culture in economics ", in *Compilation of background studies commissioned as part of the preparation of the European report on culture and development.* CMC (95) 3, Council of Europe, Cultural Policy and Action Division, Strasbourg.

McLaughlin, J. (1990) *Building a case for arts education: an annotated bibliography of major research,* The Kentucky Alliance of Arts Education.

Phillips, L. (1997) *In the public interest : making art that makes a difference,* Comedia, London.

Robinson, K. (1995) " Education in/and culture ", in *Compilation of background studies commissioned as part of the preparation of the European report on culture and development.* CMC (95) 3, Council of Europe, Cultural Policy and Action Division, Strasbourg.

Robinson, K. (1997) *Arts education in Europe : a survey,* Council of Europe, Cultural Policy and Action Division, Strasbourg.

Willis, P. (1990) *Moving culture,* Calouste Gulbenkian Foundation, London.

Williams, J. (1995) *Arts and education: a taxonomy of possibilities,* British American Arts Association (speech, Grahamstown, South Africa).

Our creative diversity: report to the World Commission on Culture and Development (1996), Unesco, Paris.

The four thematic studies on the " Culture, creativity and the young " project:

Delfos, C., (Elia), in association with Euclid (1997) *Working with young people: Training of artists and teachers*. CC-Artsed (97) 7, Council of Europe, Cultural Policy and Action Division, Strasbourg.

Hill, R., in association with the Liverpool Institute for Performing Arts (1997) *The arts, commercial culture and young people : factors affecting young people's participation in artistic and cultural programmes*, CC-Artsed (97) 5, Council of Europe, Cultural Policy and Action Division, Strasbourg.

Williams, J., in association with the British American Arts Association (1997) *More, better, different : intercultural understanding and cultural diversity : the roles of cultural provision for young people.* CC-Artsed (97) 6, Council of Europe, Cultural Policy and Action Division, Strasbourg.

Wimmer, M. ; Sonuç E., in association with the Österreichischer Kultur-Service (ÖKS) (1997) *Reflecting on youth arts: towards a new framework to enable young people and the arts to come closer.* CC-Artsed (97) 8, Council of Europe, Cultural Policy and Action Division, Strasbourg.

The Research and Development Unit of the Cultural Policy and Action Division has launched a new series of publications – the Policy Notes. These are synoptic and/or comparative reports on topical issues in the field of cultural policy.

Publications:

- " VAT and book policy: impacts and issues "

- " Culture – a way forward " (Culture and neighbourhoods : an action-research project in urban Europe)

- " Balancing act: 21 strategic dilemmas in cultural policy "

- " The governance of culture – approaches to integrated cultural planning and policies " (forthcoming)

- " Culture and civil society: new partnerships with the third sector " (forth-coming)

For any further information, please contact:

the Cultural Policies Research and Development Unit
Cultural Policy and Action Division
Council of Europe
F - 67075 Strasbourg Cedex
E-mail: decsrdu@coe.fr
Tel.: +33 (0)3 88 41 36 48
Fax: +33 (0)3 88 41 37 82

Sales agents for publications of the Council of Europe
Agents de vente des publications du Conseil de l'Europe

AUSTRALIA/AUSTRALIE
Hunter publications, 58A, Gipps Street
AUS-3066 COLLINGWOOD, Victoria
Fax: (61) 33 9 419 7154
E-mail: jpdavies@ozemail.com.au

AUSTRIA/AUTRICHE
Gerold und Co., Graben 31
A-1011 WIEN 1
Fax: (43) 1512 47 31 29
E-mail: buch@gerold.telecom.at

BELGIUM/BELGIQUE
La Librairie européenne SA
50, avenue A. Jonnart
B-1200 BRUXELLES 20
Fax: (32) 27 35 08 60
E-mail: info@libeurop.be

Jean de Lannoy
202, avenue du Roi
B-1060 BRUXELLES
Fax: (32) 25 38 08 41

CANADA
Renouf Publishing Company Limited
5369 Chemin Canotek Road
CDN-OTTAWA, Ontario, K1J 9J3
Fax: (1) 613 745 76 60

CZECH REPUBLIC/RÉPUBLIQUE TCHÈQUE
USIS, Publication Service
Havelkova 22
CZ-130 00 Praha 3
Fax: (420) 2 242 21 484

DENMARK/DANEMARK
Munksgaard
PO Box 2148
DK-1016 KØBENHAVN K
Fax: (45) 33 12 93 87

FINLAND/FINLANDE
Akateeminen Kirjakauppa
Keskuskatu 1, PO Box 218
SF-00381 HELSINKI
Fax: (358) 9 121 44 50
E-mail: akatilaus@stockmann.fi

FRANCE
C.I.D.
131 boulevard Saint Michel
F-75005 PARIS
Fax: (33) 01 43 54 80 73

GERMANY/ALLEMAGNE
UNO Verlag
Proppelsdorfer Allee 55
D-53115 BONN
Fax: (49) 228 21 74 92
E-mail: unoverlag@aol.com

GREECE/GRÈCE
Librairie Kauffmann
Mavrokordatou 9, GR-ATHINAI 106 78
Fax: (30) 13 23 03 20

HUNGARY/HONGRIE
Euro Info Service
Magyarország
Margitsziget (Európa Ház),
H-1138 BUDAPEST
Fax: (361) 302 50 35
E-mail: euroinfo@mail.matav.hu

IRELAND/IRLANDE
Government Stationery Office
4-5 Harcourt Road, IRL-DUBLIN 2
Fax: (353) 14 75 27 60

ISRAEL/ISRAËL
ROY International
41 Mishmar Hayarden Street
PO Box 13056
IL-69865 TEL AVIV
Fax: (972) 3 6499469
E-mail: royil@netvision.net.il

ITALY/ITALIE
Libreria Commissionaria Sansoni
Via Duca di Calabria, 1/1
Casella Postale 552, I-50125 FIRENZE
Fax: (39) 0 55 64 12 57
E-mail:licosa@ftbcc.it

MALTA/MALTE

L. Sapienza & Sons Ltd
26 Republic Street
PO Box 36
VALLETTA CMR 01
Fax: (356) 233 621

NETHERLANDS/PAYS-BAS

De Lindeboom Internationale Publikaties b.v.
PO Box 202
NL-7480 AE HAAKSBERGEN
Fax: (31) 53 572 92 96

NORWAY/NORVÈGE

Akademika, A/S Universitetsbokhandel
PO Box 84, Blindern
N-0314 OSLO
Fax: (47) 22 85 30 53

POLAND/POLOGNE

Głowna Księgarnia Naukowa im. B. Prusa
Krakowskie Przedmiescie 7
PL-00-068 WARSZAWA
Fax: (48) 22 26 64 49

PORTUGAL

Livraria Portugal
Rua do Carmo, 70
P-1200 LISBOA
Fax: (351) 13 47 02 64

SPAIN/ESPAGNE

Mundi-Prensa Libros SA
Castelló 37, E-28001 MADRID
Fax: (34) 915 75 39 98
E-mail: libreria@mundiprensa.es

SWITZERLAND/SUISSE

Buchhandlung Heinimann & Co.
Kirchgasse 17, CH-8001 ZÜRICH
Fax: (41) 12 51 14 81

BERSY
Route d'Uvrier 15
CH-1958 LIVRIER/SION
Fax: (41) 27 203 73 32

UNITED KINGDOM/ROYAUME-UNI

TSO (formerly HMSO)
51 Nine Elms Lane
GB-LONDON SW8 5DR
Fax: (44) 171 873 82 00
E-mail: denise.perkins@theso.co.uk

**UNITED STATES and CANADA/
ÉTATS-UNIS et CANADA**

Manhattan Publishing Company
468 Albany Post Road
PO Box 850
CROTON-ON-HUDSON, NY 10520, USA
Fax: (1) 914 271 58 56
E-mail: Info@manhattanpublishing.com

Council of Europe Publishing/Editions du Conseil de l'Europe
Council of Europe/Conseil de l'Europe
F-67075 Strasbourg Cedex
Tel. +33 (0)3 88 41 25 81 – Fax +33 (0)3 88 41 39 10 – E-mail: publishing@coe.fr
Web site: http://book.coe.fr